Have You Wound Your Clocks?

By J. S. Berman

September 2016

ACKNOWLEDGEMENTS

I would like to acknowledge my grandfather for accepting the request to write stories about his past and for being the role model that he is. I would also like to thank my grandmother for hosting us every week without hesitation and her support for this venture, without her this would not have not come to fruition.

A special thank you to my wife, Terry for her contributions, encouragement and her company at our weekly interviews.

Contents

1	Solomon	
2	Town Folk	
3	Growth Spurt	
4	Down Down Below	
5	The Learning Curve	
6	Family Matters	
7	From the Mine to the Factory	
8	A Step Back	1

INTRODUCTION

My grandfather would often tell us stories of his youth. I've always enjoyed them and find it very intriguing that he came from 'so little' and yet has accomplished so much. More often than not, we forget the past and instead of learning from it we live out our own lives with little direction. I intend to note these stories and view them as more than a little tale, rather an experience that brought about a great outcome. I strongly believe in acquiring as much knowledge of people's experiences as possible.

It's my grandfathers 80th birthday this year so I decided to tribute 120 pages to some of his achievements. I don't intend on covering his entire life, it would be impossible to fit that between two covers. Instead I'm recording snippets of an otherwise very eventful upbringing.

This writing is not a biography as it might appear to be at first glance. I'm not writing this as a book or a novel either. There is no inspiring message at the end or an epiphany that altered someone's life. This writing is simply a chronicle of short stories in order to remember a past that carved a future and brought with it somewhat of a legacy.

At the conclusion of some stories I've added my own input, sometimes just a footnote to show that paths line up or a lesson I've learnt. Sometimes it's just a thought that I had and wanted it to remain more than just a memory. I'm hoping whoever reads this will enjoy these stories as much as I did.

I'm an Electrical Engineer working at the company my grandfather started all those year ago, Switchboard Manufacturers. I recently graduated and continued with my master's degree. I married my wife Terry at the end of my third year of studies. We met in class at varsity and my grandfather always referred to us as 'study buddies'. I'm not a writer, I'm not a very articulate person but I do have the will to achieve and accomplish based on my decisions, and this time I decided to put pen to paper... or fingers to keyboard... either way, enjoy.

"I am a result of my experiences, even more so I am as a result of my history"

Chapter 1

Solomon

Sitting across from my grandfather after our regular Monday night's overly catered dinner, my grandmother suggests..., no, forces me to take another baked potato while stating "they are only quarter slices, so take a few...". She only takes one though, she claims she's been eating rice cakes the whole day.

I begin to ask my grandfather, whom I call 'Gamps', questions about his past. I wish for him to recall the moments that made him the luminary that he is today. The events that shaped his outlook on life and cut the path that he was led to follow. I ask one simple question and this is what followed...

CHAPTER 1.
SOLOMON

Meyer Feldman, or 'Cocky' as many know him, is a father of four and a grandfather of... well we don't count, but it's close to 20. He's married to Ruth, better known as 'Cookie', and no they didn't receive their nicknames in an *'Oh that couple is so cute together we should totally give them nicknames...'* sort of way, they were given to them independently in their youth and it stuck with them ever since. If anything in life is more fitting, it is these two dignitaries and their complementary nicknames.

I begin recording...

"Is the recorder sensitive enough?" he asks.

This question is the epitome of his nature; the correct procedure must be followed to accomplish the greatest outcome. If I had written him a letter accompanying a gift he would correct the spelling before taking note of the content. Not to say he is a perfectionist, or to compare him in any way to the obsessive-compulsive German nature. Naturally, as a Jew born in the 1930's he never took a liking to the Germans, so much so he landed up marrying one. He constantly reminds us of this anomaly.

CHAPTER 1.
SOLOMON

His father, Solomon, born in Latvia in the town of Riga and mother Tanya, from Bulbanova, always referred to it as *"Der heim"* - *their home*, but constantly made to feel as though it was not. Much like the Jews from Lithuania and Germany, Solomon and Tanya felt the effects of anti-Semitism during the advent of communism after the 1st world war. Solomon was drafted into the white army who were an anti-communist force fighting against the Bolsheviks, subsequently he was drafted into the red army which was established after the 1917 Bolshevik revolution. It got to a point where he didn't know who he was fighting against anymore.

Jews in Latvia didn't have much choice when it came to *Yidishkite* as they were made to attend *Yeshivas* and *Cheders* and had no other form of education. This was the law at the time. Many discarded religion all together upon leaving Latvia. One can't blame them after the travesties that they went through. It can be hard to once again put faith in the one watching over after it appears as though he was not.

Solomon and Tanya had a son named Ronnie born in 1926. Soon after in 1929 Solomon left to South Africa on his own leaving his wife and son behind. He worked with his brother in law, Robert, on a farm in order to send money back to *"Der Heim"*.

CHAPTER 1.
SOLOMON

Robert was a tall man with a farmer's presence and coming from very little religious background he was confused by the sight of Solomon's morning ritual which included *Tefillin* (phylacteries). He questioned Solomon's actions but after gazing upon a man with such faith in G-d after having to leave his wife and children behind, he too decided to don *Tefillin* from that day on.

Eventually Solomon had enough money to purchase tickets for his wife and son to board a ship heading for South Africa. They were apart for six years and reunited in 1935. At this stage Ronnie had spent most his life without a father and saw him as a man who had abandoned his mother, from a child's perspective, this is understandable. Ronnie was a tiny boy when he came to South Africa and it took him many years to warm up to this stranger who was his father. But, had Solomon not brought his family to South

Figure 1.1: Robert.

CHAPTER 1.
SOLOMON

Africa, they may have perished in the war much like many other Jewish families that stayed behind.

Tanya's sister fled to Israel and was one of the early pioneers in the region, she married there and had two sons. Subsequently her husband left her and many years later after the toils of a difficult life she took her own by jumping off a building.

My heart skips a beat as he states this with no change of expression on his face. Israel is supposed to be our end point, our goal, our Zion. It's our safe haven where we can run when the times are bad and our cities have uprooted us. And now he is telling me she went there and never found her peace...

CHAPTER 1.
SOLOMON

The Petrol Crisis

World War II began in 1939 leading to a petrol shortage in 1941. As there was a very limited supply, the public was issued petrol rations or coupons allowing them to purchase the required quantity. The only problem was Solomon and Tanya never had a car and weren't allocated a ration book.

"But why would you need petrol if you don't have a car?" I ask...

"You still need to get around..." He replies.

If you wanted a lift, either by taxi or if you knew someone with a car, you would have to contribute ration slips.

"Money couldn't buy petrol!" He says with a startled look on his face.

Pilgrims Rest, where they lived at the time, had no trains or busses, but there was a taxi service. By 'service' I mean a middle age lady by the name of Mrs Schmidt who owned a car and employed Solly as a driver. But it was only a matter of time before they ran out of ration slips. Poor Solly.

CHAPTER 1.
SOLOMON

Side Note: King Solomon son of David was credited for building the first temple in Jerusalem, and the smartest person to have ever lived. My second name is Shlomo, the Hebrew of Solomon -My younger cousin is also Solomon named after my great grandfather. Coincidentally their family driver's name is Solly which is short for Solomon.

CHAPTER 1.
SOLOMON

The Watchmaker

Solomon was a watchmaker by trade but wasn't very good at it. Sometimes he'd repair a watch and other times he wouldn't.

At this point I must mention that my grandparents' house is full of antique clocks. Grandfather, countertop, wall mounted, pendulum. I often feel that the only reason we are invited over for dinner is to wind up the seven day clocks. Each grandchild has a clock to wind and Cookie knows who forgot to wind theirs that evening and she will subtly remind them until they do. Upon starting the story of the watchmaker the grandfather clock strikes 8:00 pm. We must now wait for the eight bells to chime before we can continue...

Often people of the town would bring their pocket watches, Zobo was the make, in hope that it would be repaired, but Solomon didn't enjoy the work he did and never got around to it. In order to support his family he began purchasing odds and ends and selling it from his store. Sometimes clothing, sometimes sweets. Whatever he could acquire at the time. The only problem with sweets was that Cocky would take a handful to share with his friends and leave very little for the store. His favourite was the chocolate logs.

CHAPTER 1.
SOLOMON

He still likes his chocolates. My brother and I are currently working at the company he started 50+ years ago. Every now and then he gets a chocolate for himself and buys two extra boxes so all the office staff can get one as well. This is his nature, no matter how far up he gets, he never forgets the ones below.

CHAPTER 1.
SOLOMON

The Shoichet

As Solomon was a religious man he required kosher food and any meat that is to be eaten must be slaughtered in a kosher manner. With no *Shoichet* in the small town, Solomon had to get permission and training to do it himself. He purchased a *Hallaf* - a large knife for slaughtering and set up a chicken coop out back.

I can only assume it took practice and I'm not sure how this took place but as a new man to the trade he was unaware that upon cutting the head off a chicken it would continue to move about. So after a few attempts he appointed Cocky as the chicken runner who would chase the headless chickens round the coop and bring them back to his father. I can imagine the site of a young boy chasing after a headless chicken while his father was readying the next one. With him being the only *shoichet* in the town, there were plenty of chickens to *shecht*.

Fish was also somewhat of a delicacy in Pilgrims and Tanya being the entrepreneur that she was would buy the fish, fry it and sell to the townspeople. I'm not quite certain how the fish actually made it all the way from Kalk Bay to Pilgrims Rest without a refrigeration truck. But I know they did use dry ice accompa-

CHAPTER 1.

SOLOMON

nying the payload to keep the fish fresh. How fresh it was when it eventually arrived was masked by the spices used in Tanya's cooking.

The only time Solomon ever got angry was when it had to do with food. The only time he ever gave cocky a hiding was when it was lunch time and he refused to eat. It was the biggest sin. Food was in short supply and you were not allowed to do that.

If ever he came back from the shop after a day's work and supper wasn't ready he would start whistling. This was a hint of sort to get Tanya moving. She was also working the whole day by the way. But if she took too long he would huff his way into the kitchen, take a frying pan and two eggs and make scrambled eggs. Then you knew he was furious. Full of steam. This was the only time he ever cooked or did anything in the house for that matter.

Funnily enough my dad does a similar thing. If my mother is somewhat delayed with supper, he will make himself an egg as if to say "See, it's not as hard as you make it out to be".

CHAPTER 1.
SOLOMON

The Mohel

The eighth day in a boy's life brings with it the *Bris Milah* (circumcision) ritual, where a *Mohel* (the one who performs the procedure) is required. Cocky was born in the mines hospital and eight days later the *Bris* was to take place. Now obviously this is a delicate operation and an experienced *Mohel* is always preferred. But Pilgrims Rest didn't have a *Mohel*. They had a *Shoichet*...? but that could get messy. So they made the call. And by 'made the call' I mean booked a call from Pilgrim to Johannesburg which was routed through Middleburg, this could take between 2-3 hours, sometimes even till the next day. The *Mohel* was summoned and had to take a train and a taxi just to get there.

Naturally, Cocky doesn't recall the procedure...

CHAPTER 1.
SOLOMON

The Bank Manager

The bank manager, Tim Taylor was his name, *"The miserable swine"* as Cocky calls him, would never honour his agreement. At that point in time, you could pay by bill over 60 days but after presenting it in the bank, they would send it straight back. One couldn't buy stock for one's store.

But Solomon was a survivor and he bought what he could. This time it was suits to resell, perhaps someone needed one for *Shul.* He only had enough money to buy a few suits, so sizes were very limited. The number one rule when buying clothes for someone else, 'always buy a bigger size', this way they can make it smaller if needed. So the limited number of suits that Solomon had in his store were all of the larger variety and when someone would come in and try one on, Solomon would pinch the back of the jacket and tell them *"It fits like a glove"*.

Solomon would then send his customer to the only tailor in town, Tin town to be precise. An elderly black man who could make two suits from the material left over.

"Oib der shuch past, kenst im trogen" - If the shoe fits, wear it

CHAPTER 1.
SOLOMON

The Gifted

The busiest time in the shop was just before Christmas where all the gentiles, white and black, would need to buy gifts. Tanya was a shrewd woman and with her knowledge of the townspeople and what they'd want to buy for their wives and kids, she would take a trip down to Joburg and purchase everything on her list. Then she would head back and sell it all in the shop, each item to its specific unassuming bidder. They would sell out every year. This was their magnum opus.

The shop however wasn't always a hit. Tanya's shop competed against all the other little shops that lined the cobbled street.

Being a mine town most of the customers were labourers who's wages were paid at the end of the week. The only time people had money to spend was on a Saturday. This poses a great dilemma for those that wish to be Sabbath observant as one has to close one's shop on the Sabbath. It caused her a lot of frustration.

"Gebroteneh teibelech flien nit in moil arein" - *If you want something you have to work for it*

CHAPTER 1.
SOLOMON

The Shul

At the height of Pilgrims Rests prevalence, it had 15 Jewish families living there. As every Jewish neighbourhood needs a *Shul*... actually they need two *Shuls* so one of them can be the one they don't go to, but anyway... A *Shul* needed to be built and it was commissioned out of corrugated iron. It consisted of two small rooms and a toilet out back. This Grand Synagogue attracted the Jewish families from as far as 22 miles away. Graskop and Sabi provided another 18 families.

The *Shul* was built like a Church with a high pitched roof. Zeida, as Cocky refers to his father, would lead the service and another little man *"Even shorter than me"*- Cocky says, by the name of Yisroel Myers would help out sometimes. They had a single *Torah* and a few *sfarim* (Jewish Books).

By the time Cocky was ready for his *Bar-Mitzva*, there weren't enough Jews to make a *Minyan* in the *Shul* and they had to go to Sabi to pray there. Even so, he had to run around looking for men to join so he could read from the *Torah*.

A point to note, there is no mention of Ashkenaz, Sfardi, Lubawitch, etc... Just Jewish, that's all that was required. That's all that was available.

Figure 1.2: A shop with a plaque labelled "Feldman's", Pilgrims Rest.

Chapter 2

Town Folk

Cocky was born in Pilgrims Rest, on the 20th September 1936. Pilgrims Rest is a small mining town in Mpumalanga, it was the second of the Transvaal gold fields. It is now a provincial heritage site and a tourist attraction. I have visited there myself on a family holiday, yes we do plenty of those. It's a quaint village with corrugated iron dwellings, cobbled streets and not much else. There were two 'hotels' for passer-by's, a synagogue, a bioscope and a school. The townsmen worked endless hours in the mines and had very little to show for it.

Cocky and his parents lived in a small house at the foot of a hill with not much more than a place to eat and a bed to sleep. Cocky begins to describe the size of the kitchen by showing the measurement in reference to the dinner table we are sitting at.

CHAPTER 2.
TOWN FOLK

"From that chair over there to the end of this table, and about as wide..."

A wood stove filled up most the space available and eventually an old fridge was purchased, but as it didn't fit in the kitchen, Cocky's room was the next available spot so that's where it went. He recalls falling asleep to the grunt and hum of the fridge who became his companion from then on.

"It was an apology for a bedroom" he says

He had a shelf as a bookcase and a six inch nail on the wall - That was the wardrobe.

"What did you do in the winter?" I ask

The wood stove in the kitchen provided the warmth in the winter. But that was in the kitchen, his room remained the ice box.

Corrugated iron housing, located in a valley, near by a river, that's a recipe for a cold winter.

Cocky doesn't speak much about Ronnie, when I asked where he

CHAPTER 2.
TOWN FOLK

was during all this it took him a minute to recall.

"Oh.., he slept in a rondavel next to the house, there was no space for him inside."

There was a 10 year age gap between Cocky and Ronnie and they had very little interaction. Ronnie left when he was old enough for high school as there was no high schools in Pilgrims rest. Cocky was only four at the time so they didn't get to spend much time together.

After the description of the living quarters it is apparent as to why it is necessary to document his past. Had he have been able to foresee the man he would one day become, in the house that he would one day live, with the family that he would one day raise, he would never have believed it were possible. A young boy from a small town, now in this grand multi-storey marble home.

Their house is a large townhouse in the middle of the Jewish neighbourhood called Glenhazel. Where property prices are ballooned and a Jewish mom's biggest stress is running around on a Friday afternoon searching for Challahs for Shabbos. True first world problems exist in this Shtettle.

CHAPTER 2.
TOWN FOLK

The Bucket System

In contrast to our lavish Glenhazel homes, in Pilgrims, if you wanted to use the toilet, you would head on outside past the rondavel, up the completely uneven steps, climb up all the way to the top of the hill where a lone cubicle sat near the chicken hock. An old rooster and a few of his friends lived there. Right up in the mountain, that's where William the houseboy slept, if you think the kitchen was small, you should see William's room.

There was no light along the way. At night you needed a torch and sometimes it would rain. The water would then rush down the slope and by the time you made it up the hill, you wouldn't need the toilet any more.

The toilet was a bucket system, if you can call it that. The village counsel would send a very special wagon called the night cart. It was drawn by 16 oxen. They would arrive every night at midnight to change the bucket.

The backing of the toilet had a cut-out where the bucket could be removed and then replaced with a new one. One of the problems is that if you were sitting on the toilet at the same time as they were removing the bucket, you didn't have a very comfortable experience.

CHAPTER 2.
TOWN FOLK

The toilet being a wooden shed became appealing to the broody hens during egg laying season. They would then sit next to the bucket and when it was almost time for the chicks to hatch they would pick at your buttocks. Making your toilet experience even more 'pleasurable'.

Sometimes there were turkeys up in the hill. They were the best watch dogs. Anything coming in, a snake or a person and they would make a terrible noise. So upon hearing the noise, Solomon would send Tanya to go take a look.

One day there was a hell of a storm. The wind blew and they heard a crash. So Solomon said to Tanya *"Geyn kukn khvats gesheenish..."* - *go look what's happening.* The whole of the front balcony was gone, he can't remember where it landed but it was just gone.

The chickens remind me of our family trips as a kid when we would go for a weekend to Sun City. Wild Birds roam freely and a certain blue crane, standing at about 1.2 m tall, would chase my cousin biting at his rear. This bird was referred to as the "Bum-biter" from then on.

CHAPTER 2.
TOWN FOLK

The Doctor

Pilgrims didn't have many options when it came to medical facilities, they did however have a very good doctor, Dr Spierwater, he was great. He never needed an anaesthetist or any other form of assistance. By "needed" I mean "used". Every operation was single handed. Tanya was living proof of this. She had at least four operations done by him. She even had her Gallbladder removed.

In those days they used ether to put the patient to sleep. Cocky says there's nothing worse than his experience with ether. It takes you weeks to recover from the 'anaesthetic' and you'd have the taste in your mouth for the weeks following.

There was no dentist in the village. Doctor Van-Der Skaif travelled in every six weeks from a small town called Leidenberg. When he'd arrive the whole primary school would line up for a check-up.

Now obviously he didn't have time for any silly things like fillings or anything like that. So when it was your turn you went in, you'd sit on his chair and he would ask *"Waar is it seer?"* and you'd point and say *"Hier dokter"* and before you could take your hand out your mouth he had whipped the teeth out. There was

CHAPTER 2.
TOWN FOLK

no time for nonsense like injections or anything like that, that's why most the kids in the village had half their teeth.

Adults were in the afternoon.

That was the medical care. There was a mine hospital where doctor Spierwater performed his operations. Tanya new it well.

There was a chemist as well, owned by a Jewish gentlemen Mr Steckle. He made his contribution and meds were readily available from him.

Today it's a bit different, something such as a headache requires a Neurofen, two Stopayne, a Zomig and a Napflam. If that doesn't kill it, take a Ponado and call me in the morning. A trip to the dentist without sedation puts you in the same league as a war veteran. Only the war veteran never had to make small talk with cotton wool in his mouth.

CHAPTER 2.
TOWN FOLK

The Night Cart

Returning to the Christmas theme, there were two hotels in Pilgrims rest. The Royal Hotel and The Pilgrims Hotel. Their names slightly disproportionate to their entities yet the highlight of the high holidays was the annual Christmas lunch at one of these fine establishments.

All the gentiles would get dressed up with their wives and kids and head on down to the luncheon. Dessert time provided pudding fun where the kids would search through the desert for their Tikkies (Three pence).

Only this year was different, the night before, the fellow leading the night cart began his celebratory schnapps a little early and led the cart straight into a ditch in front of the Pilgrims Hotel. The night cart overturned and spilled its contents in front of where the lunch was to take place. As it was Christmas day, the street cleaners were off duty and the mess couldn't be removed till the following morning.

Not the most enjoyable lunch one could have.

CHAPTER 2.
TOWN FOLK

The Sukkot festival is one of the three main Jewish festivals throughout the year. We are required to eat in a temporary makeshift home to detach us from the physical indulgences of life. This temporary 'tent' is usually erected in the garden and sits on the grass, but as it coincides with the summer season in South Africa, my mother often finds it necessary to lay down compost in order to help her prize roses flourish. Eating a meal with a whiff of manure in the background is not the most enjoyable lunch one could have.

CHAPTER 2.
TOWN FOLK

Figure 2.1: The Royal Hotel, Pilgrims Rest.

CHAPTER 2.
TOWN FOLK

The Lawyer

There was a time when Solomon had to make a decision. He paid rent on his shop in the building that he occupied but the owner George Lewis, an elderly Jewish man, suddenly passed away. His son Meyer Lewis was in pilgrims and had his own shop. But now he wanted Solomon's shop for himself. It looked like there was no real will left by the old man. So they said they're going to put it up for auction. Whoever bids the highest, gets it and the money goes to old man George Lewis's estate.

So Solomon and Tanya were in dire straits, they would have to vacate. On top of it Meyer Lewis was friendly with Dougy Blane the only lawyer in town, they were big pals. Any bid Solomon put in, the lawyer would just tell Meyer the value and he would offer a bit higher, even a pound. Tanya would not accept this as being fair so she took herself to Pretoria, a place she had never been. First she went to the station, then to Johannesburg, and then on to Pretoria, but English *'she not a speak to well'*.

She eventually found the offices of the master of the Supreme Court. How she landed there and how she got in nobody knows.

Every will in this country has to be vetted and checked by this office. She was determined. She wouldn't come back until this

CHAPTER 2.
TOWN FOLK

was resolved. She saw a senior person and explained the story. They've been in the shop since 1939.

He said *"My dear lady..."*, he took to her. *"You have the right to be there. How much can you raise?"*.

That's where the problem came in, they didn't have any money. She came back with a figure that she had to raise and if she could do that the master of the Supreme Court would give it to her and ignore Dougy Blane.

It was Sunday morning and Cocky was little and his dad got a haversack and set off for a trip up the mountain. The two of them walked for miles. It was hot and far and Cocky didn't know where the heck they were going.

They landed up at Mr Teal. He was a money lender for lack of a better name. Solomon knew him because he brought watches to him to fix. He lived in a little house right up-there away from the villages. The reason he lived so far is because he married a black lady and if he had stayed in Pilgrims he would have to be arrested. The Sergeant knew him and didn't want to arrest him so advised him to live there.

It felt like hours sitting there, but in the end he lent Solomon the money on the agreement that he would have to pay him back every month. They came back to Pilgrims and put down the de-

CHAPTER 2.
TOWN FOLK

posit from the money they had borrowed and the building went to the Feldman's.

He tried many other Jewish people prior to Mr Teal and couldn't get a penny out of them. But only because of the 'old lady' he managed to get it right.

Meyer Lewis's and Cocky's parents didn't speak for the next ten years, they weren't happy with him because of all this.

In the end while Cocky was at university, he came back on holiday and got the two families together. There were six Jewish families and two of them weren't speaking. This was not ok, so he got them to make friends again and they had a little party.

There were very few Jewish children in Pilgrims. Cecil Meyers was the only one. Cocky didn't have any Jewish friends, he didn't know what Jewish girls even looked like.

CHAPTER 2.
TOWN FOLK

Old Scotty

Scotty owned a big shop down the road from the Feldman's, about 2 km away. He used to contact Solomon on the house phone which was quite new to them. One morning Scotty rang for Solomon but there was no answer. He rang again but still nothing. Scotty got worried thinking something must be wrong.

Scotty was a tall fellow with long legs, so he took a run all the way down to Solomon's shop. Upon arriving he saw Solomon sitting at his desk fixing watches and to his left, about a foot away, was the telephone.

So he said to Solomon, *"Did you not hear the phone ring?"*

Solomon said *"Yes"*,

"Then why didn't you answer it?" Scotty replied.

"Because it rings all the time"

Solomon was laid back and not too worried.

CHAPTER 2.
TOWN FOLK

A 'Knight' out

Travellers used to come by every so often. 99% of them were Jews travelling for business. They stayed in the hotels. Some were friends of Solomon and Tanya and they would eat meals with them. If there were enough of them they would have a poker game.

So who played? Solomon and Tanya, Sgt Simington, Mnr Duplesie the headmaster – old doop, old man Meyerson, a traveller and Issac Aronowits. That way they had a school of seven. They didn't fool. They would play till two in the morning, in the middle of the week and then they'd drive home.

One night when Cocky was a child, he woke up and his parents were nowhere to be found. So like the brave 'man' that he was, he put on his little gown and he walked and walked to the Dressens house. He was very little. They said they were going there for a short while. When he arrived they saw a little man standing there in his little gown. They were playing Rummie but now realised it was getting late and had to head home. So they disbanded the game and called it a night.

Figure 2.2: From left - Senta and Ernest (Oupa) Cahn, Tanya and Solomon.

Chapter 3

Growth Spurt

Cocky lived up to his nickname at times and Tanya, being the firm mother that she was, would use a belt to discipline him. He could read the look on her face the moment before she went in search of her belt. Often enough that he would try hide it in a pre-emptive response. However, this was to no avail as she would simply snap a twig off a tree and use that instead.

His dad never hit him, only once when he never ate his food. Food was sacrosanct, you don't play with food. Tanya did the *klapping* and it never stopped.

When she would give him his birthday party all the little "*Yoks*" at primary school would arrive at their porch. There was

CHAPTER 3.
GROWTH SPURT

no bakery in pilgrims so she did all the baking. They did justice to it. It was their highlight.

School was a slightly different. They never had homework. There was no such thing. He went to school *kaalvoet* – barefoot, they'd walk there and back and upon arriving home, eat and meet their buddies up the creek. All the way up the mountain opposite the house. They'd play until Tanya sent William to come find them. This happened every day.

The mountain side is a beautiful area. On the one side of the creek there are 13 streams carrying trout. The road travelling up to the mountain crosses the creek 13 times.

Tanya wouldn't let Cocky swim there until the first rain had come. The public pools were fed by the Blyde river, so if there was no rain then it wasn't clean enough to swim and had to be flushed out. The worries of a typical Jewish mother.

As small as it was, everyone knew everything about everyone in Pilgrims, much like any Jewish community now. Cocky had a friend Rex Skea. Rex had a stepfather.

Unfortunately in the war Mr Skea Senior was injured and as a result couldn't have children. An Afrikaans chap, Piet de Beer, a fine fellow who collected nuggets in the streams, fathered Rex.

CHAPTER 3.
GROWTH SPURT

No one was supposed to know about it and the only people who did know were the whole village.

Rex's father was alive and he was a priest for the Roman Catholic Church. Rex was Cocky's best friend. He grew up with a terrible complex about his father and kids would tease him saying *"That's not your real father"*. Cocky was the only person who befriended him and he would come wait outside Solomon's shop. They'd go riding their bicycles together after school.

As they grew up cocky told him that when they finish school he must leave pilgrims, he must get out. So he took his advice and left to Pretoria and managed to find a job there. It was the best thing he could have done. He then met and married a Dutch girl, a very nice girl.

Rex was complex as a result of his upbringing and used to stutter. After he left pilgrims, he had children and moved back to Graskop. Somehow he managed to buy a petrol filling station and then another one in Bushbak Ridge and a third somewhere else.

This fellow who was an outcast developed a wonderful life for himself. Financially he did very well but in order to do so he had to remove himself from that stigma.

CHAPTER 3.
GROWTH SPURT

Another friend that he had was John Boyes, a big chap who was retarded. He would meet him after school at Jonny Grievers place. Jonny was a coloured man, a shoe cobbler, he had a tiny place with his assistant. Cocky would meet John there and they would squeeze in after school.

John was a genuine 'backward'. The guys would tease him and he would chase them away when he could. But Cocky and him were good friends; he had confided in him and would talk to him.

His parents struggled with him. In those days you couldn't have a 'backward' person in the family, you would have to hide them away. But John would wonder around. He'd wait for them to finish school. He could play some games and this would help him fit in. Not sure what happened to John, but eventually his parents moved away.

CHAPTER 3.
GROWTH SPURT

We Make Enough for Everybody

There was a gentleman by the name of Mr Myerson, a big fellow, he'd visit from the Graskop area to play Klaberjas with Solomon. He had a nasty habit of never wanting to put petrol in his car. He would drive to the last drop. Sometimes he'd get stuck in the middle of the night on his way home.

He was also a very bad driver... or a good driver but only in a straight line. On one occasion, he left the Feldman's residence and while heading down the street he had trouble turning. He managed to overcome his trouble, right into the Feldman's shop. Half the roof came down and in the commotion he sped off.

Somebody spotted him and the news got back to Solomon and Tanya, they didn't say a word. They were however very friendly with the sergeant of police, Sgt. Simington, so they told him to give Mr Myerson a little scare.

The police arrived at Mr Myerson's shop and said *"We believe you had a bit of an accident last night"*, to which he responded, *"Me? Never"*. They then asked if they could have a look at his car and upon inspection it still had the paint marks from the shop roof. He got into a panic and said it can't be him. Naturally they let him go without a fuss.

CHAPTER 3.
GROWTH SPURT

I've always wondered where my grandfather obtained his love for Klaberjas. He taught his grandchildren how to play and gets a proud look on his face when he sees them doing so. It must be a sense of nostalgia for him.

Cocky landed up working for Mr Myerson, he had a big department store, big by pilgrims rest standards. His main customers were the black people from the lowfeld. Back then there was an entrance for the whites and a separate one for blacks. You couldn't go through the wrong one.

At this point Lina, the maid, is called to clear the dinner table... Oh, how far we've come.

Cocky was a little guy and during the holidays he would man the entrance to earn some extra pocket money. They had a chap in charge near the black entrance by the name of "Seventeen". Cocky was watching him closely as he clunked away at the old cash register. He was serving a black lady with a fantastic amount of parcels yet the register showed very little activity. A little here, a little there but he could clearly see they were pinching. So he ran as fast as his little legs could carry him all the way to Mr Myerson's office on the white side. When he got there he caught his breath

CHAPTER 3.
GROWTH SPURT

and told him the story.

"Seventeen and a customer are pinching you out of house and home!" Cocky said

"Yeees.." Mr Myerson replied... *"We make enough for everybody"*

Cocky looked, his eyes opened wide, he couldn't believe what he just heard... Then why on earth was he watching them? They might as well carry out the whole shop!

But Mr Myerson always paid him a couple of shillings at the end of the week. So the work was worth his while.

On a completely irrelevant note, Mr Myerson could never keep a wife. She always ran away from him.

CHAPTER 3.
GROWTH SPURT

The Driver

Cocky was crazy about driving, but never had a car to fill his desire. The closest he could get to a vehicle was the pilgrims rest garage. One could hire a truck that was used to fetch the goods that came by train to Graskop. Solly would man the truck and Cocky would catch a lift during the holidays. Every now and then Cocky would nag Solly to let him drive, so much so that he would actually let him.

When the Feldman's, Lewis's and Dressen's went for picnics by the river, they would rent that same truck with their trusty driver Solly. He would also help set up the braai. Cocky took full advantage of this and would take the truck for a bit of a spin off-road. That's where he learnt.

CHAPTER 3.
GROWTH SPURT

When we were kids, my Gran would often take us to school in the morning. She drove a two door red Mazda MX6. We lived in observatory and school was in orange grove. One day she pulled in to a quiet road and said "You are 12 years old now correct?" I said yes, she said "Well it's about time you learn to drive". So I hopped in the driver's seat and began my first lesson.

Chapter 4

Down Down Below

The mines were the heart of the town and everything thrived off them. The Traansvaal Gold Mining Estate (TGME), close to where he worked, had a recreation centre that boasted sporting facilities and a bioskope. The centre was so avant-garde that one day they made a big announcement that the following Saturday they were going to have an official opening of the first flushing toilet in Pilgrims Rest. All the 'pickaninnies' from the primary school gathered down by the WC and everybody had a turn to pull the chain and watch the water spiral down. This was a big and exciting day in Pilgrims, I wouldn't be surprised if a memorial stone was erected in its honour.

Just above the recreation centre they had the tennis courts

CHAPTER 4.
DOWN DOWN BELOW

and a bowling green. Interestingly enough, Pilgrims had a rugby and tennis team who played league. The man in charge of bowling was Meyer Lewis and the president of the rugby club was Isaac Aronowitz, two Jews leading the squad. At the club they even had two full size snooker tables.

Cocky played tennis during the holiday and attended all the round robin competitions. The bowlers also used to play in Nelspruit and Whiteriver as well as Sabi and Graskop. They would travel long distances to compete in sporting events. A five ton open-top truck would be the form of transport and could carry two teams. This was all good and fine going to the games, but on returning Cocky and the driver were the only two sober ones of the lot. There was no shortage of beers after the game. These *Chataisim* drank themselves to an absolute frazzle and they got home when they got home.

CHAPTER 4.
DOWN DOWN BELOW

Cocky still loves his tennis, and by "love", I mean "obsesses over".

We recently went on a family holiday to Zimbali for Passover. We stayed in a beautiful hotel off the beach with all the facilities one could think of and all the food one could eat, which we did. The deck overlooks an Olympic size crystal blue pool amid luscious green shrubbery surrounding the Bali style luxury villas. Beyond that is the ocean meeting the skyline in an ombre semblance.

While the rest of us prep for a relaxing day at the pool embracing the opulence as well as scheduling the exact meal times (just in case we might be 3 minutes late for lunch), Cocky dons his white tennis shorts and takkies ready for a game of doubles.

CHAPTER 4.
DOWN DOWN BELOW

Coco-Loco

In order to bring the gold ore down to the reduction works where the refinery process could take place, there was a whole series of coco-pans. These networked all over the mountains on railway tracks. In order to get it up the mountain they used electric locomotives. They were small but could push 20 to 30 trucks.

After the ore was mined, it was sent down the shoots where it filled the coco-pans. On the way down they didn't need an engine as it used gravity to get going. So for fun the kids would jump on the back of the pan and race it down the hill. It would go at an alarming speed. They were thrown off many times and there was a huge risk of getting killed, but as unwary kids they would play there every day.

"Did you ever go to the streams to pan for gold?".

You always had old prospectors and they used to sit all day in the creek while the water was washing down from the mountains. Those little rivers would wash down nuggets of pure gold that don't need refining. They were very valuable. In fact the mine had a chap, an Afrikaans guy, he had five or six men who would go looking for nuggets. They would collect them and store them

CHAPTER 4.
DOWN DOWN BELOW

in a glass bottle and hand it in to the mine. They were absolutely honest. That was their job.

The man in charge was as honest as the day is long. Ironically he retired with very little money.

Cocky and his friends would fool around with a sieve filtering sand and water in hope to find a nugget. They never found anything, they didn't have the patience anyway.

CHAPTER 4.
DOWN DOWN BELOW

Die Lisensie

Years later, when Cocky was a student, he would work during the university holidays.

Soentjie De Beer headed the mine workshop. Cocky learnt a heck of a lot in various departments such as blacksmith, jack-hammer, electrical and general motor mechanics. Cocky would service the Alvian Trucks that carried the gold ore to the refinery and reduction works.

Often it would rain a storm and the Jeeps would track through the mud. It was then his job to lie underneath and remove thump or fix a broken support.

So it was time to get his driver's licence and who was the assessor? None other than Soentjie De Beer. So Soentjie figured he's going to teach this "Engineer" from Johannesburg a lesson. Soentjie didn't like it that his whole life he worked as a motor mechanic and here a young man leaves to Johannesburg and returns bearing a degree.

So during the licence testing, he made Cocky drive up a steep hill and pull off in an Alvian truck... while in reverse.

He was a nice chap, this was just a bone in his throat. Cocky passed the test and was rather chuffed. Soentjie didn't care about parking because in pilgrims rest there was no place to park; wherever the car stopped that's where you left it. So from there he got his *"lisensie"*.

CHAPTER 4.
DOWN DOWN BELOW

Initiation

Everyone's fear when starting a new chapter in life is how you are going to fit in, how you are going to adapt to your new environment. Often this adaptation is accelerated by means of an initiation process. The mine workshop had an initiation process of their own. All the men and ladies from the offices would line up in anticipation of the new recruit. Cocky being the young rookie, had to run 100 meters in front of them *"heeltemaal kaal"* - completely naked. But to top it off, he was smeared with tar. The mines used to tar their own roads so they had plenty of it. All the women were there shouting and laughing, they were the worst.

Cocky spent a lot of time underground in the mines with a crew of blacks from Mozimbique. He learnt to speak Shanga, Sutu and some Zulu. Not many Zulus were around that area. He also picked up Fanagalo which is used as the common tongue or Lingua Franca between the various dialects.

Underground however, was a different kettle of fish. It mostly consisted of Afrikaaners and some German foreigners. He worked on city deep and was shocked to find two Jewish miners. One of them was very shrewd or at least he thought so.

CHAPTER 4.
DOWN DOWN BELOW

Jack hammers were used to cut away at the reef and at the end of every month they would measure, in fathoms, how much the crew had progressed and pay them accordingly.

So it came to measuring time and this Jewish guy, very different to the *Yoks*, put out a big table of fruit and chicken to try persuade Cocky to measure more than what his crew had cut.

Cocky tried to explain to this 'idiot', that it didn't matter if he gave him more now, that the reef had a finite area and in the end he would still get the same amount. This was way over his head and he stuck to his guns and insisted on pushing for a higher value. At the time he was an old chap. How he was still alive he's not sure because Cocky thinks this man had Typhus from the mine. Even so, it was a pleasure to meet another Jew.

CHAPTER 4.
DOWN DOWN BELOW

The Descent

The mine descent was an adventure on its own. The first stage consisted of a skip with three compartments one above the other. The *'shwartse'* would pack themselves in and the skip would lower a level for the next lot. Sometimes he was forced to go in the bottom layer.

These guys were proper gentlemen and they would urinate from the top compartment onto the people below. *"They were Pigs!!"*

But that was the more gentle part.

Next stage was an inclined shaft much like an escalator with a box to sit in. One level after the other down you go and at each stop the next crew gets out.

The more smutty crews would fill their hats with water and as your cart passed they would pour it on your head just for fun. They were the scum of the earth. And if you didn't like it they would *donner* you. They were the mine bullies.

If ever you tried to resist these guys they would make your life hell. They formed the southern suburbs gang. It was a handful of big white ugly *Boere mense*. They knew who was a Jew boy and they'd pick a fight with him. They weren't fussy who they fought with. You couldn't complain. If you went to the mine captain they would make your life a misery.

CHAPTER 4.
DOWN DOWN BELOW

The mine uniform consisted of a vest, shorts and bum and knee covers but by the time you got down to the working place you would have to change your vest. It was quickly apparent what the bum covers were for. You had to slide through tunnels 18 inches high. If you were claustrophobic you didn't have fun. To add to the beauty of the situation, you had mine water dripping on you all the time. Not just any water, acid water from the minerals in the ground. The mines tried for years to purify it but they never could. For drinking water you had to bring your own bottle.

It was boiling hot down below. The miners went down at 5.45 am and came up at 4:00 pm. Every time they went down they cursed the mine but as soon as they got back up and saw the sunshine they forgot how rotten it was and went back the next day.

If you had a break you went nowhere. You would just go to a place for free air. Lunch break you went to a station with more air and a light. If you weren't too tall you were fine, those that were couldn't stand up. The only light one had was a forehead lamp and they worked lying down on their side.

Cocky did sample and survey. He would cut into the reef and take samples which the office would then check and measure for

CHAPTER 4.
DOWN DOWN BELOW

gold content. All day long new samples and then new measurements. When he came up at 4:00 pm he would plot everywhere he had mapped. For plotting he used a theodolite which stands on three legs much like the one used for quantity surveying. It's a tough job trying to find a beacon with no light and then having to plot it in 3D. This way the mine knows which section has been mined out.

Two of the main bosses were Jewish. Mr Heller and Mr Rapaport. They were very nice to Cocky. He got into trouble at one point and they helped him out.

He had to go to an appointment in the afternoon but you can't get up till 4:00 pm so he decided to take a dip, and the only skips that were going were carrying the ore. So he jumped on one. This is quite dangerous because as it gets to the top it tips.

Needless to say he got caught doing this and it was reported to the mine captain. He called him in and gave him hell. As the punishment for the next couple of weeks he worked in a development section, which was right at the bottom of the mine where there are no facilities. For air there was a single pipe and the heat was worse than before. But because of Mr Heller and Mr Rapaport who pleaded his case he wasn't kicked out. This all took place in final year varsity so he really needed this job.

CHAPTER 4.
DOWN DOWN BELOW

One day without any notice, the mine closed down. They couldn't find the reef so they closed it up. Everyone had to leave, the party was over. Cocky's parents had the shop with all the goods and they had to sell it. Luckily the Transvaal Provincial Administration decided to turn Pilgrims rest into a heritage site otherwise they wouldn't have gotten a penny from the sale. A price was decided and it was expropriated.

It was Cocky's final year at university and in-between prepping for exams he had to bear the burden of relocating his parents, which didn't go so well. They were short of money and he was short of time. On top of this, his dad had to find a job in order to pay rent. He finally found a spot in a barber shop in Yoeville. There was a small table by the window and he would sit there doing what he did best, be it not so well... fixing watches. He then managed to get a job as a *Shamesh* in the Burea *Shul* from 5:00 – 8:30am, came home for breakfast and then went on to fix watches.

It was a very difficult time for them. Cocky would come home every day and help Solomon count how much he made that day. They battled. Cocky had a job lined up for the following year, but he landed up failing a subject and had to carry it over to the next year. I assume the constant attention to the relocation had a lot to do with it. So while he studied, he went to work in another mine in order to make some sort of income. He wasn't very excited

CHAPTER 4.
DOWN DOWN BELOW

about it but they paid reasonably and with the money he made he managed to help out his folks.

He emphasised how tough it was for them at that time.

Zeida eventually worked in Cocky's factory sorting and issuing bolts. About the workers, he said *"They all crooks"* and wouldn't give them a thing without requisitions.

One day he was late for work and cocky was driving. He shouted *"Why you going so slow we going to be late!"*. Cocky said there are cars in front. Zeida said *"These blady Portuguese, they're rubbish!"* Cocky said *"How do you know he's Portuguese?"*. He said *"He must be, look at how slow he's driving"*.

A *'Bissle'* racist he was.

One day they were getting into the lift in Alfreda Mansions where they stayed, a black man, 'The flat boy' got in with them. So Solomon leans over to Cocky and says in Yiddish *"Vos tuter doch"* - *What's he doing in the lift?* So Cocky replying in Yiddish says *"Hes going up to the 4th floor just like us"*. So Solomon said *"Hy kan gey mit der trep"* - he can go with the steps".

CHAPTER 4.
DOWN DOWN BELOW

It's a running joke in the family that those who start working at the factory begin by sorting nuts and bolts. It's a mundane job but someone has to do it. I didn't realise that it was actually true. I guess this is where it originated.

Figure 4.1: Miners on their lunch break.

Chapter 5

The Learning Curve

Cocky attended high school at Athlone Boys in Johannesburg and boarded at the Herbert house. King David School wasn't around then. He went on to study at the University of the Witwatersrand.

He applied for law and was accepted. He wanted to become and advocate. So he arrived for registration and stood in a long line to register. It didn't matter which faculty you belonged to, one line fits all. It was a lot less formal back then. At the last minute however, just before he got to the front of the line, he changed his mind. He'd like to do Engineering.

So the professor said "Feldman, how can you do engineering".

He said "Why?"

CHAPTER 5.
THE LEARNING CURVE

The professor replied "Your marks in maths and science are lousy!"

One was a C and one was a D or something along those lines. He told the Professor that because he knows he's weak in those subjects, he will work double as hard in them. He knows that he is down for law, but he's decided that he's not interested.

Years later he figured out why he changed and realised that he would never be able to defend someone who he knew was guilty.

He began first year Mechanical Engineering but ran out of money so he continued to work underground in the mines for another year. He battled throughout. In July he got a job at Motor & Diesel repairing crank shafts as well as grinding valves and pistons for cars and tractors. Pinky Gale fixed him up there.

He then worked in the kitchen of the Doll's House off Louis-Botha and started the Northern babysitting club at wits. He printed flyers and gathered some good customers. Other students joined and it became quite popular. It wasn't a large income but it was some sort of income for the time being. He travelled around by walking or hitching, sometimes after a shift at 2:00 am. In

CHAPTER 5.
THE LEARNING CURVE

those days people stopped and it was safe to do so.

He then stayed in Yoeville at Mrs Mossleson who was an old widow, lovely old woman. She had a dog called *Daishy* (Daisy) and a worker named *Tomash* (Tomas).

Often summer time brought with it thunderstorms in the afternoon and it would begin to get dark as the clouds blew over. Mrs Mossleson in her old age would think that it was almost night time and call Cocky for dinner.

Cocky - *"But Mrs Mossleson it's only four o'clock."*
Mrs Mossleson - *"Yes, we must go to sleep now."*

She was also hard of hearing so there was no winning.

He would have to eat supper at four o'clock in the afternoon and head to bed. He was boarding with her so he didn't have much choice.

In final year, he plugged fluid dynamics and had to repeat the whole year. It was a silly system, it still is. He couldn't write a sup so he worked for the next year and could only go back two years later.

He worked hard at varsity but physics gave him trouble. He

CHAPTER 5.
THE LEARNING CURVE

managed to scrape through maths. When all the guys would go out on a Saturday night, he would be studying. He didn't find it easy. At the time there was only one choice of Engineering, which was Mechanical. In final year, Aeronautical Engineering was an option but it was a waste of time in South Africa because the only company to work for was Denel. He did board in Mechanical Engineering designing steam and diesel engines.

Figure 5.1: Cocky in his graduation gown.

CHAPTER 5.
THE LEARNING CURVE

Disorderly Conduct

During the holidays, Cocky would road trip to Maputu (Lorenza Mark) and had to cross the border at Komartipoort. Only they went through on motorbikes. One guy had a Nash sedan and nobody had money. With nowhere to stay they slept on the beach. Some had straw mats to sleep on, others did not. Either way everybody had a good time. Cheap flask wine was the drink of choice and boy did they make the choice to drink. The Penguin night club was not short of entertainment and some of the boys even started messing around with black maidens. They weren't allowed to do this in SA so this was seen as quite a rebellious feat.

Cocky tells me he went home at 3:00am, by home he means the beach. The others arrived a little later drunk and by 4:00am he woke up drenched. The tide had come in and by squinting his eyes at first light he could make out the silhouettes of haversacks floating away. The drunk coots didn't even notice a thing and it took them a day or two to come to light.

They got in a bit of trouble and as they were leaving. The sirens could be heard in the distance. Disorderly conduct was not tolerated in that part of town. It was a very strict country. The police were sharp. One could leave one's belongings unattended

CHAPTER 5.
THE LEARNING CURVE

and no one would dare touch his stuff. But it was a cruel government. If one was caught pinching they would chop off a finger. Any worse and it would be a hand.

CHAPTER 5.
THE LEARNING CURVE

Slow Mo -ped

While he was studying in JHB, someone offered him a little mo-ped, a half breed between a scooter and a motorbike but not as powerful as either. He was excited and paid it off bit by bit. He took it home with him on holiday. It was small enough to fit in the train from Lidenberg, about 60 km from Pilgrims. From there he got off the train with his luggage and a large grin on his face. The plan was to ride this mo-ped back to pilgrims. But about two miles in on the dirt road, the mo-ped gave a tut... tut... tut... and a clunk. The bike conked out. It wasn't meant for those types of roads, I don't even think it was made for the road. So he hitched from there and someone with an old flatbed put it on the back and he made his way. He was lucky to make it home.

Eventually he got an old 'Royal & Field' motorbike. He would go riding with the boys Sunday afternoon and kept the bike by his parents while he was studying in JHB. On the next visit home he asked his mom "Where's my motorbike?"

She wouldn't budge.

"Where's my motorbike??" getting a little more distressed.

CHAPTER 5.
THE LEARNING CURVE

She finally cracked and told him.

The miners used to walk to work in the early morning, you could hear their gum-boots marching on the cobblestone. So she stopped one or two of them and asked if they wanted a motorbike. They said "How much?" and she said "Five pounds" and a deal was done.

She didn't care if she got one pound out of it, she said "No ways you driving a motorbike. You can get hurt or killed" and that was that.

He didn't even get to keep the five pounds.

CHAPTER 5.
THE LEARNING CURVE

It must be Fate

Once he qualified as a Mechanical Engineer, Cocky worked for Norman Fate Impacts. His first job was manufacturing tubes. The kind used for toothpaste and makeup. They were made from aluminium but later on they started using plastic.

He recalls an interesting tube that they got an order for that was used for a product called 'Artra'. The tube had to be made of lead. Nothing else could hold it. Artra eats through anything, even aluminium won't do.

A well known Jewish family was in the pharmaceutical business. They manufactured all kinds of medicine and chemicals. They would fill this and sell it to the blacks for whitening and lightening their skin. This would eat away at their skin and eventually lead to cancer. They sold it for years until it was finally outlawed. They made a lot of money from it; it was so popular in those days because blacks had nothing. The lightly coloured had a little more so they would try their best to lighten their skin. Journalists have never forgotten this little story. Any chance they get at this family they'll have a go because of it.

So Cocky worked there for a year and a half. The company was sold to a new group and Cocky wasn't happy with them. Norman Fate left and Cocky soon followed. He then joined a company

CHAPTER 5.
THE LEARNING CURVE

called Fuch's Appliances. They manufactured washing machines, stoves and circuit breakers. He worked there for four and a half years.

He worked in production in the transformer section. He had an excellent Jewish boss by the name of Chup Rothwall. You never made a mistake twice with him.

Chup said to Cocky *"Do you want to learn? Then you will do what I tell you"*.

Every morning, Chup would walk through the factory and have everything written in his little book. He took no nonsense and knew everything. He remembered everything as well. He told Cocky when you walk through the factory open your eyes and observe. He could pick up anything out of the ordinary. He was a strong teacher and Cocky learnt a lot about production from him and even more about people.

Just before he joined the company the big boss, Eljay Jacobson, retired. A big chap, genius but peculiar. His son David became the head of the Counsel for scientific and Industrial Research (CSIR). In the morning, during winter, he would walk around in a large overcoat and a hat and suss out what the guys were up to. One morning he saw something that annoyed him; he removed his

CHAPTER 5.
THE LEARNING CURVE

hat threw it on the floor and stamped on it. At that stage every supervisor excused themselves to the toilets, there was no one to be seen. He then proceeded to stomp through the factory.

Cocky knew the welder, a very good welder, a bit of a boozer, didn't have many brains.

One of these wild mornings when Eljay was 'cooking'. The welder came up to Eljay and said *"M...M... more menier Jacobson"*.

"More!" - Morning

"Asseblief, can ek die welding machine koop?" – *can I buy the welding machine?*

Jacobson turned round and glared at him and said *"Vat die donger se ding!"* - *take the blady thing!*

"H...H...Hoeveel menier."

"Ek se, vat die ding!" – *I said take it!*

There was no cost, and he walked on. He was a bit cuckoo but he built an enormous business.

CHAPTER 5.
THE LEARNING CURVE

Cocky had another Jewish boss by the name of Cyril Frankel Fooks, a proper German. He started a factory making pots and pans, one section made specialised equipment for the defence force. He would visit each section every day but he started developing arthritis in his later years. He was so crippled by it that they had to help him get into his car. He landed up selling it to Barloworld.

He was clever, in all key positions he employed only Jews. He had no children but he had a rule that the highest any of his family members could go in the business is dispatch clerk. No higher in fear of them destroying the business.

I'm glad Cocky doesn't have the same mentality as Cyril, or else I would be counting bolts for a living.

CHAPTER 5. THE LEARNING CURVE

Figure 5.2: Cocky and Cookie (Left)

Chapter 6

Family Matters

"Were there any significant turning points in your life?"

There was a turning point in his life when he met this young lady - pointing at Cookie. It was when he was shoved into marriage. Cookie then kicked him into touch. She stopped him from playing rugby on *Shabbat* and other funny things like that. So that was a major change in his life as it is in all our lives. He said it was a turning point but he didn't say it was a *lekker* one.

Cocky met his wife Cookie oddly enough at a *Shiur* where they were introduced by his future brother in law Sonny Wilk. Sonny was dating Lotty, Cookies sister, who he eventually wed. Sonny persuaded Cookie to come with them as there were poten-

CHAPTER 6.
FAMILY MATTERS

tial *Shiduchim*.

Cocky sat next to Sonny in the Yoeville Shul. They attended the Shiur by Rabbi A.H Rabinowits. Cookie saw Cocky asking questions and he seemed quite intelligent so she agreed to meet him. The thing about Cocky is that the moment you meet him, you have an instant liking towards him.

Cocky and Cookie started dating in November of the year 1962. On their first date Cocky took Cookie to watch him play soccer. A helpless romantic he is. It was very interesting having her there because he saw her when they arrived and again when they left. He took her out a couple of times to play hockey as well.

They got to know each other and he came to visit her when she had her wisdom teeth removed. She was all bandaged up and in a bit of pain. To his surprise, he found an 'ex' boyfriend of hers visiting and what seemed to be at that stage was that he didn't see himself as an ex. He was all sympathetic (*I sense a bit of jealousy in his tone*). Cocky wasn't too sympathetic, he's not the sympathetic type.

CHAPTER 6.
FAMILY MATTERS

The Question

Cocky went on holiday to Cape Town with four or five of his mates. They stayed in Sea Point on London road. They hired a small flat and needless to say they had a very nice time. Cookie was in Muizenberg, the *Shtettle*, at the same time. It's about a half an hour drive so he went to visit.

Lotty and Sonny had just gotten married and he came to the airport to visit Cookie. Then cocky was invited to a very special lunch by Cookies father, Ernest, or Oupa as we knew him. They had been dating for about six weeks at the time. The lunch took place at the Imperial hotel. It seemed to be a very nervy lunch, everyone was a bit jittery and not very relaxed.

Before half way through, Oupa said that he wants to go for a walk. It's an odd thing for him to do during the middle of the meal. Cocky reluctantly agreed to go with him as he felt he should.

So they walked outside up and down the side walk quite briskly. Oupa never did anything slowly. Cocky looked to the side where the window of the dining room overlooked the street and he saw Cookies family peering through anxiously waiting to see what's happening.

CHAPTER 6.
FAMILY MATTERS

Oupa said *"Listen, you've been going out with my daughter. We don't mess around."*

Cocky said *"What do you mean?"*

Oupa - *"You've been going out for six weeks, what's your story?"*

So Cocky replied again *"What do you mean?"*

Oupa - *"Either you're interested or you're not."*

Cocky said *"Look we have to get to know each other still, I can't make any decision now."*

Nothing was concluded there, he said he would get back to him and he left Muizenberg as quickly as his feet could get him to the car. He's not sure if he saw cookie again that holiday. He was petrified.

CHAPTER 6.
FAMILY MATTERS

I've never known my grandfather to make rash decisions, in fact he's quite the opposite of rash. I had a similar encounter with my father-in-law. I came over to my wife's house for a visit but she wasn't home yet. This was before we got married. I saw her father sitting having lunch and before I could make a run for it, as I had a feeling that this was bad timing, he called me over to come join him. He asked "What's happening with you and Terry?". Like my grandfather before me I responded "What do you mean?" He said "You've been dating for four years, you are 'frum', when are you getting married?" This was now an unavoidable question. We then settled on a date at the end of that year which I had been considering prior to our discussion. Only now it wasn't a consideration, it was a request for permission

CHAPTER 6.
FAMILY MATTERS

The Engagement

Cocky got back to Joburg and the pressure was on. He had to make a decision. His mother was around and he knew he'd have some trouble with her so he told her that he was dating someone. She wasn't happy about this at all. Then she met Cookie and they all went to a movie. The moment she found out she was German, she took an instant dislike towards her and that was that.

So to keep the peace Cocky would drop his parents off every Saturday night at a movie and then go fetch Cookie separately and head back to the same movie house.

Cocky tried to persuade her to give Cookie a chance. He wanted to know why she wasn't fond of her. The truth is, whichever girl he would've brought home she would've disliked. But Cookie was not only *Frum*, she was German! This was no good.

He then told Tanya that he's getting engaged. Whether it was genuine or an act, she was now fainting all over the place and somehow mustered the strength to say that she will never accept it.

Ronnie, his brother who was married to Jean, liked Cookie and he intervened. He worked on his mom and helped calm her down. That was the first hurdle.

CHAPTER 6.
FAMILY MATTERS

The engagement in itself was a bit of a laugh. It was an afternoon tea with a lot of people. It was called for between 2:00 pm and 5:30 pm at 32 Observatory Avenue. Oupa looked at his watch, it was already 6:00 pm so he started chasing people out. He was German so punctuality was everything. He stood up and said it's enough. An elderly couple walked in and he said it's too late and shooed them out.

So it was a very happy courting time with Cocky dodging the blows. Either Cookie was unhappy or Tanya was. Oupa and Senta, his wife, didn't interfere after they had collared him.

Figure 6.1: Ernest (Oupa) and Senta Cahn

CHAPTER 6.
FAMILY MATTERS

The Wedding

So then they needed to set a date for the wedding. 17 June 1962 was chosen. But Tanya being Tanya said she's not coming to the wedding. Ronnie sat with her and Solomon till two in the morning persuading her to come. Solomon never got into arguments, he kept quiet, he had no chance against Tanya. She finally agreed to come and I'm sure conditions had to be met.

Oupa called Cocky and said you must decide what you want for the wedding. An afternoon tea, an evening wedding or a morning wedding. If you have an evening wedding, you won't have any furniture. If you have a tea, we will get you stuff for the kitchen such as a fridge and a dining room suit and beds. Cocky said he will discuss it with Cookie and without much discussion they agreed on an afternoon tea because they needed the furniture.

They didn't have too many guests as his parents didn't know anyone. The Cahn side, Cookies family only had the *Yekkers*, a really happy mob. The wedding was a tea, hot or cold any as you please.

They wanted to get married in Beria Shul as Solomon was the *Shamesh* there. Drama followed as the *Yekkers* wanted Rabbi Zaltzer, the old man, to marry them. But Rabbi Zaltzer said that

CHAPTER 6.
FAMILY MATTERS

he won't marry in the shul because there was an old organ upstairs where the choir stood. No one even knew how to play it. It had been there for decades but he wouldn't marry them as it was *"Goyish"*. So a hum-and-a-ha later Rabbi Alloy and Dr App, an old German who wasn't too friendly, agreed to marry them.

At the wedding Cookie didn't start crying nor did Cocky, but Tanya did. Sobbing. She thought if she cried enough she could swim away in her tears. Everyone thought she was crying out of happiness but they were very wrong. Ronnie was very upset with her. There is an 8 mm film of her sitting there, donned with a large purple hat, her face white as the wedding dress itself. Any donkey could see this was not a happy woman. Cocky had to dodge the hail stones once again.

For some reason she fought against everything religious. The *Mikvah* was too dirty she said. I think coming from a place with so much persecution against Jews she was somewhat dissuaded from what seemed to be the cause.

This was a wedding to be remembered. A little different to the ones in recent years but with much the same drama.

They then went to stay in the Cranbrook hotel which first became kosher and then eventually became a brothel. Cocky says he was a bit early as he only got the kosher version. It was right

CHAPTER 6.
FAMILY MATTERS

in the middle of Hillbrow.

They didn't have Sheva Brochas - The seven blessings that are given to the couple during meal times. It wasn't as popular in those days.

CHAPTER 6.
FAMILY MATTERS

The Honeymoon

Happily, they got into their Renault Dauphine and drove off to Durban. On the way, near a place called Nottingham hill, Cocky hears 'click click click...' He stops the car and gets out. The left front wheel bearing had packed up. Right in the middle of nowhere. The inside bearing on the axle was shot. So he jacked it up and could see some of the ball bearings had fallen out. He proceeded to put them back one by one and smeared it with Vaseline. This somehow managed to keep the bearings in place and he then put the wheel back on. They drove very slowly until they reached Pietermaritzburg. They found a mechanic and he asked what's wrong with it because it now looked fine. Cocky told him but he said there's nothing he can do. So off they went to Durban on three and a half wheels. It's a far route up and down the hills but they finally made it and got a replacement part from the agent.

Cookie went with her mom to a sale at John Awes before the honeymoon and the fancy dresses they bought never fitted. Now she has a thing about going to sales. I don't think this has had a positive effect on Cocky's credit card.

Cookie had two dresses for the whole honeymoon. *"Whatever you need your husband will buy you"* they said. She says she's still waiting. Cocky says she's still collecting.

CHAPTER 6.
FAMILY MATTERS

They stayed at the Menora hotel. Next door was the Hilton Heights, a nice block of flats that became a kosher hotel. When they walked into the breakfast room all the oldies whispered amongst themselves *"Ooh, a honeymoon couple"* so much so they wanted to jump out the window. Even so they had a nice holiday in Durban away from everyone.

Upon returning from Durban, cocky went straight to work as he always does. Cookie did a dress designing course and then she found out that the clothing factory where she worked didn't want her back. They kicked her out and she went to work at another place that made trousers. It was a very boring job but it was a job. They lived in Houghton Ridge on the corner of Dunbar and Cavendish street in a one bedroom flat. It was very small but had a big balcony.

Lotty and Sonny also stayed there and they had wonderful neighbours by the name of Desawer. Then Lotty moved into a little house in Dunbar Street. The old people bought a house for them in upper Houghton after that. It was a shocker though, she hated it. Lotty wished that the oak tree would fall on the house and smash it. But her *Sheitle* would save her, Cocky says. Then they moved to 212 Observatory Avenue where Manny, Cookies late brother, took over when they moved to Israel.

CHAPTER 6.
FAMILY MATTERS

Manny was 13 years old when Cookie and Cocky got married. He was a wild one. Getting older he wasn't interested in getting married, he wanted to travel. He went overseas a lot. He went skiing and broke his leg, came back to get it set and returned to skiing. His parents went *Shidduch* hunting and no one was good enough. Eventually Lotty found Dina who he landed up marrying. He was 31 years old when he got married. He would come over when cocky would play poker and bring his friends and Cookie would make them steaks. It kept her going because there was nothing else to do in the flat by herself.

Cookie left for work every day at 6:45 am to catch the bus in Cyraldine. She left before Cocky did. Two years later Adi was born and she decided to start teaching swimming lessons. She would take Adi with the maid who would look after her. Cookie bought a Cortina with the money she saved which eventually was put up as collateral for the factory.

The schools would come to Cookie for lessons, Rabbi Bernard sent the Menora Oxford boys and then the girl's school. Observatory girls would come in different classes at different times. The beauty of all of this is that no one ever paid.

CHAPTER 6.
FAMILY MATTERS

Figure 6.2: Girl's swimming lessons 1975

Figure 6.3: Boy's swimming lessons 1975

CHAPTER 6.
FAMILY MATTERS

Sundays were nice... for Cocky. He played hockey in the morning and soccer in the afternoon. He visited his mother after, without Cookie, then played poker in the evening. That's what kept the marriage so fresh, he says. *"Rubbish!"* Cookie says, she was lonely. It was a lonely period in her life. She took the kids to swim at her parents when he was out all day.

Now days Cookie isn't as well known for her swimming lessons as she is for her Mayonnaise and Gewickelte-kuchen. What is Gwickelte-kuchen you ask? Well it's the most German a cake can get and has the ability to last for several years as long as it is wrapped in tinfoil. Don't ask how I know this. As for the mayonnaise, it is the best mayonnaise in Joburg. Many have tried to replicate it; none have succeeded...

CHAPTER 6.
FAMILY MATTERS

The Trek from Germany

Oupa and Senta Cahn came from Germany. Oupa's father, Menachem Cahn, was an antique dealer. He was very clever; he said a Jew and his money never live in the same country. He had seven children but prior to the war his wife and one child died before Oupa's *Barmitzva*. He brought up six children on his own.

He had money for each child in a different part of the world. So when Oupa saw things going south in 1933 he left to France where his money was and lived there for four years. When they released his money he got ready to board the next ship out but it happened to be *Yom Tov* at the time and he refused to travel as he was observant. All his friends boarded and he was left behind. He was so depressed that for the first time in his life he got drunk. The ship got torpedoed and there was not a single survivor.

He then took the next possible ship out which happened to be travelling to South Africa.

Cookies mother, Senta, was in Holland studying dress design. She came from a village called Sontra. She went back to her parents in Germany to persuade them to come with her to South Africa. They were the last Jews to leave Sontra as they refused. They said *"The Germans would never touch us look who we are"*, they were the *Burgemeisters* - the mayor and mayoress.

She chose South Africa because her cousins, the Hallbrums and

CHAPTER 6.
FAMILY MATTERS

Carlbergs, were living there in Springs at the time. Her mother was a Levenstein and her sister married a Louinstein in America.

Oupa and Senta met in South Africa at a Jewish boarding house run by Mrs Cohen. After two weeks they were engaged and married. Cookie asked him how they could do something like that so soon after meeting. He said *"We were two lonely frum Jews who had nothing... so we had even less together"*.

Eventually Oupa opened up a bicycle shop and went to learn at night in the library on how to manufacture paint. He then opened up a big paint factory with Mr Lunce. They called the company ULAC. Lunce had money so he set them up and Oupa ran the factory. They made paint and putty for windows. Every time there was a hail storm he was happy; he would run to the factory and turn on the bore mill and ready the raw material. It was their busiest time, the next morning they were flooded with orders because all the windows were smashed from the hail.

They had a big fire once where the varnish caught alight. Insurance paid out but it was a horrible event.

Manny studied a BA and went to work at the factory but it was too mundane for him. He was smart and innovative. He tried new things like silicon but the core business was paint and putty. It was a good product.

CHAPTER 6.
FAMILY MATTERS

They developed a candle light in a tin for restaurants but the stuff they used was smelling and didn't light. They sold the product before perfecting it. It was a failure. They even opened up a resin plant but that didn't work either. The core business was neglected and the company was deteriorating.

Oupa was getting old and unfortunately the company went under. After so many years this was tragic. He was about 78 years old and had to retire. He had been in the business for 46 years. He didn't want to stop working but he didn't have a choice. Cocky put in over R1 million at the time to try revive the company but it wasn't enough. When Oupa stopped working it was the worst for him. He wasn't the same.

Oupa would take his old Jaguar to Muizenberg. He wouldn't let go of it. It would get stuck every day and they would have to push it. But they couldn't convince him to get rid of it. He loved it. He was very bright but in his old age he started forgetting things and couldn't drive any longer. Senta was very sharp. She had two strokes but nothing could stop her. She quit smoking at the age of 87. The doctor told her to stop and she did. She also kept the family *Frum*. There was no nonsense with her.

They did have money overseas and he put away enough to live off. Senta bought a flat in Israel after Oupa passed and she lived out her days there.

CHAPTER 6.
FAMILY MATTERS

The First Born

Cocky was 46 years old when he opened up the electrical factory in Germiston and some would call him a bit of a workaholic. Cookie was heavily pregnant with Adi, her eldest, and Cocky dropped her off at Florence Nightingale Nursing Home, opposite the Hillbrow prison, he then left to work at the factory.

Sometime later, after not hearing from his wife in labour he decides to call and find out if she had given birth. Something must be happening by now he thought, so he called the nursing home and they put him through to maternity. He asked if Mrs Feldman has had a baby yet. They asked who's speaking and he said her husband. They then said, *"We can't tell you anything, if you want to find out you have to come to the hospital"*. So he had to tear himself away from the factory to visit his wife and newborn.

Luckily Cookie didn't wait for him to give birth to Adi or she'd still be waiting. For Sean, the second eldest child, Cocky also didn't make it there but for Howard and Alon he delivered them, which Cookie says was a bit creepy. I tend to agree.

Cocky was involved in the Menora Oxford school which was run by Rabbi Norman Bernard at the time. That's where his kids

CHAPTER 6.
FAMILY MATTERS

attended school so it was his contribution. He was the chairman there for seven years.

Simultaneously, he was the chairman of the Yoevile Shul and that went on for 30 odd years when the Shul eventually moved to observatory as the crime picked up in the Yoeville area.

After leaving observatory to settle in Glenhazel, he decided to take a back seat and let the younger people look after the Shul businesss. He was also very much involved in PTA activities at all the schools that the children attended. Jokingly he says he learnt how to embezzle the funds and that he is still living on the proceeds.

A school print from 1975 regarding the tenth anniversary of the Menorah Primary School reads:

"...To our loyal and super-reliable bus drivers - old John Thathe o.b.m., then Solly [Another driver named Solly], and now Daniel, Richard and Lucas - who have, thank G-d, driven countless thousands of miles carrying our precious cargo to and from school safely. To our active P.T.A., which, under the dynamic leadership of "Cocky" Feldman, is the envy of many a larger school and organisation..."

As far as the children are concerned. He must admit he spent

CHAPTER 6.
FAMILY MATTERS

more attention to the sporting side. Soccer, hockey, tennis. Unfortuantely their children didn't participate in rugby as their mother wasn't in favour.

He tried to attend all the soccer games and he did attend all the drama shows. He says he attended ALL the debating.

Cookie interrupts by saying *"The children never did debating!"*

"Once or twice." Cocky replies.

"They did public speaking." Says Cookie.

"How would I know the difference?" He says.

He heard them mumbling on stage, he didn't know what they were doing. Either way he "willingly" attended public speaking and proud to say that their children excelled themselves. They were very active in this area. He also did whatever he could to help with homework. It was extremely difficult because he came home late and he had to visit his mom after work. This gave Cookie breathing space he says... She didn't need it Cookie replies.

He does admit, Cookie did the bulk of attending to the kids. He does want to mention that she only mentioned it a thousand times in their marriage that she wanted six children. It's still under discussion he says. But this is between them and not for the table.

Four is tough, but six...would be lovely. It seems like they do differ on some matters apparently.

Figure 6.4: Cookie and Cocky's children in their Graduation gowns. From left to right - Sean, Howard, Cocky, Alon, Adi

Chapter 7

From the Mine to the Factory

Suddenly, Norman Fate, the chief financial officer of Fate Impacts who got Cocky his first job, announced one morning that he was leaving.

"What do you mean you're leaving? You are the CFO, how do you leave a job like that?"

He said he had to leave. There was a board meeting and the chairman wanted him to sign some papers and the papers were illegal. So he insisted that if he was forced to sign the documents, he'd resign and he did. He walked and let cocky know on his way out.

As soon as cocky heard the company was being naughty, he

CHAPTER 7.
FROM THE MINE TO THE FACTORY

decided there and then that he was going to look for another job. He never found out the real story; they would buy companies and strip their assets.

Cocky knew other engineers who qualified with him who were working for Fooks in Albertan so he went for an interview and got the job. Chuk Rothbart was the big boss and he was a strict one.

The only problem was Cocky had to survive and the salary was poor. He was married at the time. He worked Sundays because he didn't want to work Saturdays in order to observe *Shabbat*. He worked there for four years and wouldn't leave work before 7:00 pm.

The salary was very low and he was struggling. So he went in to see the boss Louis Klein, a good engineer but a tough guy.

Cocky said *"Boss, I can't come out on my current salary... I'm married, I have expenses, you have to help me."*

So Louis replied *"There's nothing I can do."*

"Look, I can't make it with this current income, if it doesn't improve I will have to look for something else."

"Are you threatening me?!"

CHAPTER 7.
FROM THE MINE TO THE FACTORY

> *"I'm asking for some help, some relief is that threatening? You sit in my chair and I'll sit in yours and we'll see how you manage."*

"Well I can't do much about it."

> *"Boss, I'm telling you now I'm looking for a new job."*

Louis said *"Do so for yourself."*

(Cookie says he was a horrible man)

So Cocky looked for all possibilities. He was offered a position in a switchboard company, Halbrons in Nigel. He researched the whole industry and said it's a shocking industry and he wouldn't go into it. He looked at all other options and couldn't find anything suitable.

Oupa, Cookie's father, knew he was looking so he told Cocky about a guy named Ralph Stock, a German, he was an electrical contractor fabricating switchboards. He had a partner who let him down and he needed someone to join him.

One Sunday morning they went down to the Vaal. Cookie was pregnant at the time with Adi, her eldest. Cocky told her he is going to discuss this prospect, it will only be an hour or so and

CHAPTER 7.
FROM THE MINE TO THE FACTORY

that he's just humouring Oupa. But after an hour he returned to say he'll be a little longer. Cookie sat waiting the whole day and it turned out that he took him up on his offer.

The place was a mess. It was small and had steal lying everywhere. A couple of small machines littered the floor but none of them worked. The guy who advised Ralph knew nothing about anything. The company was 99% *'Machula'* because of it.

They didn't have many customers at that stage but for whatever stupid reason Cocky accepted his offer and gave a pledge.

But all he had to pledge at the time was his green Cortina. So he handed over the car to the company and Oupa signed in the bank for a limited overdraft. It was a small amount but that was his investment. From this agreement he was now a partner. Maybe not the best partnership one could dream of, but a partnership nonetheless.

Within the first couple of weeks Ralph showed Cocky how to wire a board and then he went home. There was an inspection the next day and he was roasted by the consultant. He never knew a thing.

Working at switchboard, I now know how pedantic some of the consultants are during inspection. Anything they can find wrong with the board, they will.

CHAPTER 7.
FROM THE MINE TO THE FACTORY

The partners got on well and Cocky started dealing with customers. They would take chances between the factory and visiting customers. Ralph looked after the money, he was very astute, a proper German and hence he was extremely difficult.

At the end of the week they had to look for money to pay the staff. On top of that at the end of the month they had to pay suppliers. They had limited capital so the growth of the company was an uphill battle.

They spent money on the broken machines and employed 20 staff. After some time they started getting more work and needed more people and better machinery. They borrowed money from the shippers. That's not too *lekker*. The shippers lock you in with high interest, terrible people. They had the bank on their case all the time. Their biggest wish was to get out of the clutches of the banks.

The game was mostly owned by Jews. As soon as the factory finished training up a new wireman, he would resign and leave. There was a chap in Switch-King, he had been there for years, Naty Shapiro. It turned out that Naty had been paying the factory a visit every now and then when Cocky wasn't there. He would send a message with his guy to call a wireman to his car and have an interview around the corner. If he was happy, he would take him on as one of his own.

Someone eventually squealed and Cocky got hold of Naty.

CHAPTER 7.
FROM THE MINE TO THE FACTORY

Cocky told him that he is aware of his tricks and who he's taken from them and the next time he comes near his guys he will *"knock his block off"*. He never did it again. He gave them a very hard time for a while though.

Cocky has never taken anyone from his opposition. If someone approaches the factory, he calls up their company and lets them know before interviewing.

It was easier to get staff back then without the unions and all but the problem they had is that the government instated job reservation. This meant that a black man was not allowed to do a certain category of work. He couldn't use a tape measure or set-squares, it was totally illegal. They fought this heavily and they were right.

The government inspector would come round and check on all the workers. One black worker was a foreman and he wasn't allowed to be. Vandermerve, the fat labour inspector would then fine them, it was big money in those days. But they had a pretty young lady in charge of issuing wages so she would go away with Vandermerve for the weekend and a R20,000 fine became R5,000 the next morning. This lady who worked for them was worth gold. Chris Maro was her name. Cocky says he wasn't allowed to go away with her for some reason.

In good time they opened up a factory in Durban followed by Protective Eastside. They had partners there, Peter Mackiber

CHAPTER 7.
FROM THE MINE TO THE FACTORY

and Jose Almeda.

A man called Shrieks worked for them and they made him manager in Durban. He didn't know anyone there though, which was a bit of an oversight. They did research to see if it was sustainable and it was and so they stationed a depot. But it was a failure. The Durbanites wanted them to be a fully-fledged factory and then they would treat them as such. So they started manufacturing there little by little until it became a manufacturer on its own.

A Depot was then started in Pretoria. But again it was a mistake. They figured Pretoria is 56 km away, why start a whole factory when they can just deliver. But if they wanted Pretoria to work they needed to be a factory in Pretoria. This seems to be a regret in the expansion process, an error in judgement Cocky says. In addition, when starting a company in an alternate area it requires managers from that area, one who knows how the people operate there. One who is familiar with the way business is conducted in order to get a slice of the action.

Cape Town followed suit. Either it was a fully fledged independent factory with all the facilities or it was nothing. South Africa differs from Europe in that sense. European manufactures have one large factory and multiple distribution warehouses. SA however, has multiple small factories in various locations.

CHAPTER 7.
FROM THE MINE TO THE FACTORY

Something that I've noticed over the year or so that I have been working at the factory is that for every project we receive or request for quotation that we get, it is always through the hand of Hashem that it comes our way.

But it doesn't stop there. Cocky often complains about the "laziness" of some of the factory workers. Not to say they don't work, and not to say that there aren't hard workers, because there are and they do. But every now and then, when a foreman or two are on leave and the decibel level in the factory is noticeably lower than the norm. A quick walk past the punching machines will tell you that nothing is being cut despite the strict deadlines that we have. A quick walk past the bending machines will tell you that nothing is being bent, despite the strict deadlines that we have and similarly in the welding section, despite... well you get the picture... but over in dispatch there are 20 odd men pushing out fully completed distribution boards which ARE somehow meeting their deadlines. This in my eyes is an open miracle.

CHAPTER 7.
FROM THE MINE TO THE FACTORY

The Whitney

The Joburg factory started in Boysens, Offertin near Gold Reef City. They got wind of a big auction sale and one of the items was a specialised punching machine called a Whitney. Cocky went down to see if he could make a bid. Before the auction started everyone had a look around the "warehouse" to see what was up for sale. They started off the auction, first up was not the machines but the property itself. So they started bidding.

"R100,000 , R200,000..." *it's going for nothing* Cocky thought. The stand was 8,000 square meters. The building was 5,500 square meters. All this for less than a million?

A couple of guys had their bids until it reached R700,000 so Cocky put up his hand... "Seven hundred and fifty thousand".

"Gone to Mr Feldman!"

What have I done... I came here to buy a Whitney.

After this Cocky ran to the corner to find a payphone. He dialled his partner, Mashe Shmookler.

CHAPTER 7.
FROM THE MINE TO THE FACTORY

"Mashe?"

"Cocky, did you get the Whitney?"

"I...I bought the building"

"The Whitney?"

"No... the building!

"Where are you?!"

"Somewhere in Wadeville."

"I'm coming. Don't move!"

It turns out this is the very building that the Johannesburg factory is currently operating out of. It's a massive property and it came with a paint shop and camel back oven as well as dipping tanks and all the air compressor piping. It was a good buy, they just didn't have the money at the time to buy it. They also had to pay to vacate the property in Offertein so it was a bit of a muddle. It stood empty for ages.

They managed to get a bond and had to redo some areas They then had to move and build office space. Mashe was a bit upset but he got used to it. By moving however, it doubled the turnover. They used the opportunity to reorganise and the new

CHAPTER 7.
FROM THE MINE TO THE FACTORY

facilities meant that they had to rely less on external contractors. In no time they expanded into it. Initially the plan was to rent out the extra space but it was filled before they knew it.

"The accidental purchase of the Wadeville factory didn't just happen, it was purely the hand of G-d that this property came by when it did and with G-d's help we were able to expand into it like a puppy growing into its skin."- Cocky

My grandfather then used the expression like a boxer hound growing out of its wrinkles. He always had dogs but most of all he always had boxers; I could never understand the appeal. Boxers are slobbery brutes with low intelligence. They were always crazy and ill behaved. As a child I would run from the entrance of their home to the front door terrified of being enveloped in mucus from those nutty hounds. The only part I likes was the names he used to give his dogs. Achmat, Chulio, Pedro, Luigi and Monte (I assume after Cookies slight obsession with Monte Casino).

CHAPTER 7.
FROM THE MINE TO THE FACTORY

The Present

Throughout the life of the switchboard factory, Cocky had five partners. Whoever left did so on good terms and with money in their pockets. He still gets on with those who are around. Why this wouldn't be the case necessarily is because in a few instances the partners left him holding the 'baby'. He was often left in a difficult position. The partner wanted to be paid out but anyone in business knows that you cannot just find money to pay out. A business needs its working capital and one can't just grab a chunk at will. It's after tax money which the company must expend because someone decided, in his wisdom, that he now wants to emigrate.

So it was always a difficult situation but he always managed to settle and they always left on good terms. Sometimes it took longer and they had to wait but the business couldn't suffer, that was priority.

Business is not easy. In South Africa in particular it fluctuates like a Sin curve. High peaks and low troughs. Business is always up and down but if you make it through the troughs you can excel in the peaks.

One way to compensate for this is to become national. Sometimes the Cape is busy while the Transvaal is quiet and they compensate for each other over time. This gives the company support.

CHAPTER 7.
FROM THE MINE TO THE FACTORY

Every company must be in the forefront of their field in order to capture their share of the market. Some companies do this by investing in reliability and other in innovation. Switchboard does both and at one stage tried their hand at low cost housing. They managed to build a house in three days. They did it over a long weekend. Finishes and all. But the government at the time weren't ready or able to provide and it dwindled. The white government weren't interested in providing for the lower class at the time.

The house cost R30,000 and was fully functional with a shower, kitchen, toilet and all. It was made out of special concrete blocks that were manufactured by switchboard and put together like Lego. They even began making foam bricks which were a cheaper light weight version of the ones used in low cost houses today. It would do very well with the right interest.

Another venture that didn't quite fill the bill was an oil separating machine. Cocky went to Manchester for a couple of months to get this innovation off the ground. It was a fantastic machine but it was too slow.

The big bus or truck depots would deposit their oil waste in big sumps. This machine would purify these deposits and pump the clean water back into the sewerage. It had to pass a purification test and then it was fine to go back into the drain. The water was

CHAPTER 7.
FROM THE MINE TO THE FACTORY

separated so precisely that you could drink it. The oil then went to the oil recyclers and if it worked the recyclers would pay for it.

They manufactured the machine and its components locally but in South Africa people weren't using it. It was too slow, so instead of separating the waste, they went out in KZN and dumped the oil there.

Legally one is not allowed to dump oil in the sewer. But with the time the machine required to separate the oil naturally and then filter it after that, it wasn't feasible. To be fair, Jose Almeda who designed this machine, never knew why the overseas systems were working and Switchboards one was too slow. Then he found out that theirs was also slow and they weren't using it. They lost a lot of money on this.

At one stage Switchboard was very big in nurse call systems for hospitals. They did the Joburg Gen, Sandton Clinic, etc... The problems with hospitals is that when one is built it takes 8-10 years and they buy one system then you have to wait till the next one is built. It's a very slow process with not much demand. They also did x-ray lighting but not any more.

CHAPTER 7.
FROM THE MINE TO THE FACTORY

I asked Cocky if he had any significant memory that stood out.

When it came to work he had a desire to be on his own. He didn't want to work for someone for the rest of his life. So when he had this offer to join Ralph Stock who's 13 years his senior, he took a chance and joined him. That was a hard slog, they had to fight with customers for money, improve products and monitor the turnover. 50 years later he's still fighting with customers for money, still watching the products and still monitoring the turnover. The only difference is the numbers have increased.

Do you have any advice for people who are developing their business?

One thought comes to mind. You have to continuously push the accelerator and then apply the break, you have to know when to do which. Either cut all expenditures or go full steam ahead. If you think now is difficult, you ain't seen nothing. The construction industry is up and down and sometimes there's no work around.

The company has never retrenched people in all their years and its hard not to. The company gets slack and people go onto a three day work. Switchboard has never had to do that. It's not

CHAPTER 7.
FROM THE MINE TO THE FACTORY

like the software industry where there's a boom and an app sells for millions. *"I've never been in that league"* he says. I just know you got to work with it and stay with it and there's stability in that and it pays.

Switchboard don't advertise at all. Even so, every single day one or two emails come through from new people that we've never heard of before. They know we have a reputation of quality and stability and after sale service.

Out of choice consultants would rather give the job to us. But often their budgets are tight and we can't work to their silly budget otherwise we would work ourselves out of business.

The other thing to mention. No matter how long you are in business there's no guarantee of anything. We've been in business for 52 years. It doesn't mean anything. Oupa said to him that after 10 years, you are established, that's all, established. You take your foot off the accelerator and you're in trouble. You have to be constant, stable and at it. You have to know everything around you. You can't just be technical or clued up with the accounting side. If you are involved, you must know every aspect; you must deal with people and build relationships.

CHAPTER 7.
FROM THE MINE TO THE FACTORY

Were you able to see Hashem's hand at work throughout your business?

"All the time. When we bought the factory it was all him and every day since. If it wasn't for Hashem's constant help I'd be running a fish and chips shop, while having to reuse the oil."

Cocky always did want to run a resort. He feels he would be a very good host, especially to the ladies. *"In case they need anything"* he says, a book to read perhaps or a tennis racket. He loves his tennis.

He always thought that one day he'd like to teach in a classroom. *"In today's times with no chance of disciplining the little rats, it would be too frustrating"*. He could only do so using the old methods.

Chapter 8

A Step Back

Another small town my grandfather holds dear to him is one that is a bit better known. The town of Muizenberg, Cape Town, is the holiday home away from home for many Jews living in Johannesburg who need a quiet time-out away from the crowds. But as everyone has the same idea, away from the crowd, is the crowd.

My grandparents have a flat in a building called Arlington Court across the road from the beach. My family have been gathering there for literally their entire lives.

For as far back as I can remember, every December we would fly down to Muizenberg for school holidays with all the other Jewish families. Arlington Court was the biggest attraction second to the beach itself. The building catered large multi-bedroom flats

CHAPTER 8.
A STEP BACK

and even maids quarters, because who else would look after the kids if we didn't have a room for the maids?

In later years, Muizenberg became more of a stop-over before an overseas trip. Where once this was the official holiday destination, it is now the secondary holiday home as an overseas penthouse holds more street cred than a Muizenberg one.

Muizenberg, or Jewsenberg as many refer to it is a beach town a stone's throw away from Fishhoek and a lengthy walk from Kalkbay. I don't really understand the attraction there, I mean..
There is a beach, and the sand is soft...
There is a sea, and the water is warm...
There is a Shul, and the choir is ...well there's a choir

But with all these attractions there's one thing that lets it down, the reason I haven't been back in so long.
The wind!

The wind, the wind, the wind...

By calling it "wind" is seems to be a cool breeze on a hot summers day. No! This is more like a tornado within a wind tunnel.

CHAPTER 8.
A STEP BACK

8:00 am on the beach can be a perfect combination of sun and breeze and by 8:05 my beach chair has reached Fishhoek.

A typical beach scene has umbrellas tumbling across the sand accompanied by a *Sheitel* or two. Good Samaritans are not those who help old ladies cross the street rather they help them catch their beach equipment before it knocks someone in the head.

But every so often, a golden egg is laid and a day arises where the sun is out and the howl of the wind can't be heard, the kids lather themselves sufficiently in sun screen and everyone heads off to find their spot on the beach. The beach talk then consists of how beautiful the weather in Muizenberg is and the moment anyone mentions the word "Wind" they are shunned because Muizenberg doesn't have wind, it never has.

I bring this up because I am here now, I'm writing this from the sea side looking back at what a vibrant town this was and in its own way still is. I'm back here on our regular family holiday only this time it's more of a nostalgic trip as I haven't been here for almost a decade.

Some things have changed, others are exactly the same as they always were. The waterslides have a new coat of paint and the putt-putt course has some repaired greens. The traffic light has a new button for pedestrian crossing and I think they replaced

CHAPTER 8.
A STEP BACK

the lifeguard's post on the beach. Other than that everything is exactly the same.

In a town where nothing lasts, this is quite impressive. Residing near the sea, everything is weather beaten. The street poles, the huts on the beach, the cashier at the waterslides... everything will be replaced. Only here when it is replaced it is not upgraded; it is repaired to fit its function in the exact same way as it was to begin with.

Maybe this is what my grandfather holds so dear to him. Even though everything around us is moving at such a fast pace, even though everything is changing, Muizenberg has always stood still. It's a portrait of itself. It is a place in time where one can stop and think and watch the kids play in the sand. This is where we spend time with those that are important to us and appreciate our true reality and not the one that we have fashioned.

And even though our beach bag inventory consist of stingose for bluebottles and spf+ 500 sun screen (the sticky one), and even though our perfect day may be ruined by the odd shark scare or two, Muizenberg will always be our destination, it will always be our holiday home away from our holiday home.

The End

CHAPTER 8.
A STEP BACK

A footnote...

You've been married for over 50 years, do you have any marriage advice for young couples?

Don't buy her anything, she's already got it.

"But on a serious note, you've got to remember, once you are married and you wanted to get married to this person, you have to be welded into one unit. Take for example Cookies background, it is completely different to mine, they're miles apart. I was a country bumpkin and she was a stern German. Her parents were Yekkers and mine Litvaks but they got on exceptionally well. Oupa made a point of it.

Figure 8.1: Cocky and his son Howard - Muizenberg beach, Cape Town.

There are times where you have to stand up to a silly quirk of the parents. Parents can interfere and get in-between and before you know it you are arguing between yourselves.

CHAPTER 8.
A STEP BACK

You must not cramp each others style. You mustn't stifle each other's interest or ways. It's very important and doesn't come in one day. You are in accord with each other. Sometimes your partner does something to irritate you and it's not on purpose and it keeps repeating but you have to be kind about it. Count to ten. Sometimes you don't know the full explanation. Even though you asked them not to do it, they've done it again. But you have to control it and find out the real story. Maybe they had no choice and with an explanation it makes sense.

No one gave me advice. The last fight we had was probably this morning or last night but remember in the end you fighting about the same thing. Much like in a business where you have partner and they would fight but the winner is the company because it's for the sake of the company. It's a common cause and therefore it must go right. Become one unit and see it for what it is. It doesn't develop in a day but it starts coming together when others realise that when they talk to either of you, its like speaking to one person.

I was not very kind. I was Boorish. I had to work. I couldn't stay home and watch her performing. I was never gentle. I had always been used to getting up at 5:00 am from working on the mines. I had to be underground by 5:40 am and needed two buses to get there. I've always been this way."

CHAPTER 8.
A STEP BACK

Do you have any advice for raising children?

"Each one is a different child. Same mother and father but each one is so different. Some are sensitive, some wait for a good hiding before they can feel better, some only respond to talking and others get away with everything.

Don't ever try and compare them. You have to be totally fair to all of them. More so when they get older and married. But it's fair according to their needs. Sometime they will get upset because they haven't been treated equally. It's not about money, it's about attention. The fact that the one is in the background makes it so very hard for them.

The other thing is they don't like secrets. They don't like being left out. It's very painful for them if they feel excluded or unfairly treated. But any normal intelligent people are natural parents, there's nothing to worry about."

They didn't know what to do with the child when they came home from the hospital. One side had to be fed, the other side had to be cleaned. That's all they knew. There was no information. There were no milestones to reference. They just did what they did when they did it. Today you know exactly what to do. All the information is on-line.

CHAPTER 8.
A STEP BACK

Anything to add?

You must always remember, your main support is Hashem. I'm no bible pusher but all I can say is if you go out into the big wide world without Hashem helping by your side, you are very brave. I find that I always get a response. I've been in some tough positions and He's always come to the party, to use a silly expression. It's only if you sincerely build up a belief. You've got to build up something and believe that He does and can do whatever you need. You meant to ask Him for things.

I always have a laugh when the guy comes to collect money and offers me a Brocha and for more money he can give a better Brocha. Who needs it? A direct line is better.

Some people with money are mean with it, they want to be rich. Top of the box. But the money is only there to help you. It's a means to an end. Money in itself is nothing. You can have billions, then cancer comes along.

"If money can solve it, it's not a problem." - Cocky Feldman

CHAPTER 8.
A STEP BACK

Figure 8.2: Cookie and Cocky (Right) on vacation in Muizenberg.

www.ingramcontent.com/pod-product-compliance
Lightning Source LLC
Chambersburg PA
CBHW071315060426
42444CB00036B/2865